Managing Leave and Attendance Problems:

A Guide For
The Federal Supervisor
(2nd Edition)

Published by:

FPMI Communications, Inc.
707 Fiber Street
Huntsville, Alabama 35801-5833

(205) 539-1850• Fax (205) 539-0911

ISBN-0-936295-35-X

Cover design by ID Marketing & Design
Huntsville, Alabama

Acknowledgements

We would like to express our appreciation to Nancy Brandau and William B. Wiley, Esq. for their efforts in reviewing and editing *Managing Leave and Attendance Problems.* Both of these people have extensive experience in the Federal employee relations field and their comments and suggestions were invaluable in putting together this book.

by

Dennis K. Reischl

and

Robert J. Gilson

TABLE OF CONTENTS

Introduction

Chapter One: Managing Annual Leave

Chapter Two: Dealing With Tardiness And Attendance Problems

Chapter Three: Managing Sick Leave

Chapter Four: Other Leave Categories

INTRODUCTION

MANAGING LEAVE AND ATTENDANCE PROBLEMS

Managing Leave And Attendance Problems

INTRODUCTION

Managing leave is an important part of the job that every Federal manager and supervisor must master. Both agency regulations and labor agreements establish a web of rules that cover a broad variety of leave situations, ranging from those that come up everyday—such as annual leave—to those that may only arise once or twice in your entire career.

Because employees usually present leave requests and leave problems directly to their immediate supervisors, you are expected to know the rules governing leave; to understand both the employee's rights and your responsibilities in dealing with leave issues; and to make timely, correct decisions on a wide range of routine questions.

For example:

• To which employees should you give preference in scheduling annual leave?

• Are employees automatically entitled to leave without pay when their accumulated leave runs out?

• When can you require a doctor's certificate to support a sick leave request?

• When, if ever, can you cancel scheduled annual leave; when are employees *not* entitled to use sick leave?

Good News/Bad News

The bad news in this is that you have to get a firm handle on a bunch of rules that cover a broad variety of leave situations. Furthermore, you need to understand how to apply them correctly in dealing with day-to-day questions that will come up.

The good news is that mastering the information you need to know is not nearly as difficult as you might have thought. Although there is a fair amount of confusion on the subject of leave management, when we look at the rules closely you will discover that they are generally fairly simple and easy to understand. And, as you will discover, even where the rules are not perfectly clear cut, you are allowed to exercise a considerable amount of judgment in handling various situations. Finally, for those tough questions that really are not easy to figure out, it is helpful to remember that every agency—including yours—has personnel specialists available to help you find the answers you need.

Purpose of This Book

The purpose of this book is simple. It is to cut through the regulations and rules and lay out—in plain English—the information you need to understand to make solid decisions on leave issues.

In doing so we will focus not only on explaining the rules themselves, but also on showing you how to apply them in the typical situations you are likely to encounter on the job.

The bottom-line objective, therefore, is to provide you with the information you need to make decisions on leave issues confidently and correctly, and to recognize the special situations in which you should seek further information or assistance from personnel specialists.

How This Book Is Organized

As noted above, there are a broad variety of leave categories. In practice however, supervisors and managers find themselves dealing most often with situations and questions that grow out of the three most common leave categories: annual leave, sick leave and leave without pay (LWOP). Taken together, these three types of leave probably account for 95% of the leave questions and problems that supervisors face.

Accordingly, this book is organized to devote the most time and attention to these leave categories. Less discussion is provided to the less commonly-used forms of leave, such as court leave or home leave.

In dealing with the common leave categories we will outline the *basic information* you need to know, then focus on the *issues and problems* that often come up, and point out your specific *responsibility and authority* in dealing with such situations. Finally, each of the major leave category chapters will include a summary of *key points* to provide a quick way to refresh your memory on important principles.

How To Use This Book

To get the most value from this book we recommend that you take the following approach to using it.

First, read through the chapters to get a good overview of the rules, common problems and practical tips on how to administer the various types of leave. This will provide the information you need to deal with the majority of situations that are likely to arise.

Later, for help in dealing with specific situations, zero in on the appropriate chapter to provide a quick review of key points. For example, if you need to deal with a grievance concerning the cancellation of scheduled annual leave, a careful review of that section of the book will prove helpful.

Finally, you will note in reading the chapters that there are several areas in which we stress that agencies have the right to choose their own approach and make their own rules. For example, agencies have different rules on the minimum block of time employees can use for annual leave. Some agencies require a minimum of one hour, others allow employees to use annual leave in as little as six-minute increments.

In areas such as these, find out what approach or rule your agency has established *before* making leave decisions. Otherwise, you risk making a decision contrary to agency policy, and unnecessarily creating a grievance or other problem.

Good Luck

We hope you will find this book interesting, informative, and above all useful in managing leave issues on the job. If you have any recommendations on how we could improve this book or make it more helpful to you, please let us know by calling or writing—our phone number and address are included in the title pages and near the back of the book.

Good luck in dealing with leave issues back in your workplace!

CHAPTER ONE

MANAGING ANNUAL LEAVE

CHAPTER ONE

Managing Annual Leave

Introduction

An on-going duty that every federal supervisor must learn to handle is managing the use of annual leave. Although that may not sound like much, it is important that you clearly understand your rights and responsibilities—as well as those of the employees you direct. Failure to do so can quickly lead to problems with work scheduling, lost leave, grievances and disputes among employees.

In this chapter we will outline the basic principles that govern the use of annual leave, clearly define your rights and responsibilities, and discuss the most likely situations you will encounter while managing annual leave in your work unit.

Basic Principles

Annual leave is a benefit that most federal employees are granted by law. In connection with the hours they work, employees earn annual leave that they are entitled to use for a broad variety of purposes. Generally, of course, employees use leave for rest and recreation or to take care of personal business.

Employees earn leave at different rates, depending on their length of federal service.

- Those with less than three years service earn annual leave at the rate of four hours for every 80 hours of work.

- Those with three or more but less than fifteen years service earn six hours for every 80 hours worked.

- And those with more than fifteen years earn a full eight hours every 80 hours. Part-time employees earn annual leave on a pro-rated basis tied to the number of hours worked each pay period.

Employees may accumulate up to 240 hours of unused annual leave (360 hours if assigned overseas), and can carry accumulated leave over into the next year. Except in unusual circumstances, however, any earned hours above that number are lost at the end of the leave year. This is known as the "use or lose" rule. Upon leaving the service, employees are paid in full for any accumulated, unused annual leave hours.

Although employees automatically earn annual leave and are entitled to use it, agency managers and supervisors have the right to schedule and control its use. In other words, although employees have the right to use leave, supervisors have the right to determine *when* it will be taken. There is no automatic right to use annual leave at a particular time of employees' choosing, and therefore employees must first obtain permission to use it.

Supervisor's Responsibilities

As a supervisor you have several important responsibilities in managing annual leave.

A Balancing Act

First, you must see to it that leave schedules are sufficiently balanced and spread out to avoid serious interference with the operation of your work unit. That means you may have to disapprove leave requests if too many people want off at the same time. You may have to disapprove leave requests if you are temporarily short of staff or if workload is too high to allow anyone to be absent during a particular period. In fact, you are even entitled to cancel leave that was approved earlier, if necessary to deal with a serious workload or staffing problem.

On the other hand, you are also responsible for making certain that employees use a sufficient amount of leave to avoid forfeiting any hours through the "use or lose" rule. That means it is up to you to stay on top of employees' leave balances and to see to it that each employee schedules enough leave to avoid year-end leave forfeitures, if at all possible.

Note that it is not necessary that you approve the *purpose* for which an employee wants to use annual leave.

The Supervisor's Balancing Act

•• You must ensure that leave schedules are spread out to avoid interference with your workload.

•• You may have to disapprove leave requests.

•• You may have to cancel approved leave.

•• You must ensure that employees use enough leave to avoid forfeiting hours under the "use or lose" rule.

Case Situation

An employee requested four hours of annual leave for the next day. The immediate supervisor asked why the employee needed the time off. When he replied that he wanted to attend a scheduled rally to protest possible furloughs of federal workers, the supervisor denied the request, remarking that the unit had more important things to do.

The supervisor in this example made a serious, but common error. She based her answer to the leave request on the employee's intended use of the time off, rather than on the unit's workload situation. How an employee will use annual leave is not the supervisor's concern. As a general rule, annual leave requests should be granted or denied solely on the basis of your unit's workload demands. If the employee can be excused without causing problems, the request should be granted.

This does not mean you should completely ignore an employee's reasons for requesting leave. A particularly serious reason for a leave request may tip the balance in favor of granting it, even though you might not ordinarily do so in light of the current workload. For example, you might approve leave to provide care for a seriously injured family member for several days even though the workload is high and you would prefer to have the employee on the job.

Following the Rules

It is also up to you to understand and apply the rules your agency has established on how annual leave must be requested and how problems are to be resolved. As you will see in this section, there are several basic leave request and approval rules you should become familiar with.

Case Situation

An employee who was recently reprimanded for sleeping on duty has requested annual leave for the Friday following the Thanksgiving holiday. Her supervisor has denied the request, commenting that the employee is already sufficiently well-rested.

What is wrong with this approach? Simply that it appears to use leave denial as an informal disciplinary action. Leave requests should not be denied or cancelled for disciplinary reasons or as punishment for poor performance. As a general rule, keep leave decisions completely separate from other issues, such as disciplinary actions or performance appraisals. If the leave was properly requested and workload would permit the employee's absence, the supervisor should approve it.

Keeping Track

Finally, it is important to note you are responsible for making certain that employees' use of leave is properly documented on a standard leave request form (SF-71) or on official time cards. In most agencies supervisors are required to sign timecards to certify that they are correct and accurately reflect the hours worked and leave used during the pay period. Occasionally time cards are audited by trained investigators, and you could be held responsible for any errors that turn up. Accordingly, you should take the time to make sure timecards are correct before signing them.

Obviously you are the most important person in the management of employees' annual leave. The rest of this chapter will provide information you will find helpful in meeting your responsibilities.

Rules for Using Annual Leave

Rules governing the use of annual leave vary from one agency to another, although the basic principles are much the same. In general, the rules covering annual leave are found in two places: Agency regulations on annual leave, and in labor agreement provisions that may apply to employees you supervise.

Annual leave rules usually set up guidelines dealing with the following issues:

▲ *Leave request procedures.*

Agency regulations and labor contract provisions usually require that employees request and obtain approval for annual leave *in advance,* except in emergency situations. That means that employees cannot count on having a request for annual leave approved unless it was okayed earlier. In short, you may turn down a spur-of-the-moment request for annual leave. If an employee is requesting leave to deal with a personal emergency situation, of course—such as an accident or illness in the family—you would usually grant the leave request unless the work situation is truly critical.

Case Situation

An employee calls in about an hour after starting time on a scheduled work day to request annual leave. He explains that he has decided to go see the circus, which is currently in town. What are your alternatives?

Answer

You have several alternatives.

a) You could approve the leave. But if you do not want to encourage further last-minute requests you may want to remind the employee that annual leave should be requested in advance, and that failure to do so could result in a denial of the request.

b) Since the leave was not requested and approved in advance, you could direct the employee to report to work. You would probably do this if you need to have the employee there, or if you are actively trying to discourage him from requesting leave at the last minute.

c) You can also carry the employee as absent-without-leave (AWOL) for any work time missed if he arrives late. (In some agencies this is called unauthorized absence or UA.) AWOL places the employee in a non-pay status, but is not a disciplinary action. Being on AWOL can serve as the basis for a disciplinary action, however.

▲ *Procedures for scheduling annual leave in advance*

Many agencies have established procedures for scheduling blocks of annual leave for vacation purposes. Under such arrangements, employees are usually required to submit requests for five or more days leave before a specified cut-off date, such as March 1st. Once scheduled, such leave usually cannot be changed to a different date without the permission of the employee's supervisor.

▲ *Leave preference arrangements*

Another feature of many agencies' leave rules is an established method of determining who is entitled to preference when more employees request leave for a particular period than can be allowed to be absent. Preference may hinge on which employee filed a request first, which has more federal or agency service, or which had first choice the previous year.

▲ *Documentation requirements*

Most agencies require that employees document leave requests for more than a specified amount—perhaps one hour or one day—by filing an SF-71 with the immediate supervisor. Even when SF-71's are not required, supervisors are usually required to reflect the use of annual leave on the employees time card.

▲ *Allowable increments of use*

Usually agencies also establish the minimum amount of leave an employee may take at one time. Although many require that employees take at least one hour of leave at a time, some agencies allow use in increments of as little as six minutes.

Case Situation

An employee arrives for work 30 minutes late. This is the third time in the last two weeks that she has been tardy for work. You have spoken to the employee about the problem previously, and want to impress upon her that she needs to get to work on time. What can you do?

Answer

You have several options.

a) First, you could permit the employee to use annual leave to cover the time. If your agency allows leave use only in increments of one hour or more, however, the employee would have to take a full hour—and you could not assign work during the remaining 30 minutes of that hour. This approach may not be effective in convincing the employee that she needs to come to work on time, however.

b) Alternatively, since no leave was requested or approved in advance, you could mark the employee as AWOL for the 30 minutes work time she missed. You would select this response if you felt the employee has been adequately warned previously, and has not presented a sufficient reason for her late arrival.

c) Managers in some organizations have the flexibility to modify an employee's shift for a day to make up the lost time—if you think the employee would be productive during this make-up time.

Note: In using AWOL to deal with tardiness be careful to treat employees consistently and in accordance with any rules set up in your labor agreement. Although you have considerable room to exercise judgment in excusing occasional tardiness, you need to treat employees in an even-handed manner.

▲ *Cancellation policies*

Agency rules also usually outline the circumstances under which supervisors may cancel previously approved annual leave. In most cases the rules indicate that leave should not be cancelled on a whim, but only in situations in which a serious change in staffing levels or workload makes it absolutely necessary to keep an employee on the job. Some agencies even require supervisors to provide written reasons for any leave cancellations.

The bottom line is that there are a variety of rules regarding leave use that you must be able to apply correctly in supervising employees. It is not enough simply to try to do what "makes sense" at the time, or what seems fair. Failure to know and apply the rules properly can quickly lead to disgruntled employees, feelings of favoritism, and complaints. If you are not sure what your agency's policy is in any of the areas outlined above, now would be a good time to find out the answers.

Common Annual Leave Problems

Supervisors inevitably wind up having to deal with a garden variety of leave problems and situations that come up in the workplace. The brief sections that follow describe the most common situations and provide guidance for dealing with them.

Failure to request leave in advance

This is one of the most common problems supervisors face. Usually it involves an employee calling in after the work day has already started to state that he or she won't be in, and wants to be placed on annual leave. It is important to realize that it is entirely up to you to approve leave or not in such situations. You are not required to agree to the employee's request in such situations, and can instruct the employee to report for work or be charged as AWOL for any absence.

Again, however, you are entitled and expected to use your personal judgment in deciding whether to grant the leave or not. If you are satisfied that the employee has a legitimate reason for the late request—such as the unforeseen illness of a child—you may grant the request. You also may request additional information—such as a doctor's slip attesting to the child's illness—to back up the request before granting leave.

Regardless of the reasons for a late annual leave request, however, if granting the leave would create a problem or if an employee has repeatedly taken this approach, you may disapprove the leave request and carry the employee AWOL for any missed work time.

Request for advance annual leave

Employees sometimes request more annual leave than they have currently earned. Some—though not all—agencies allow employees to use advance annual leave up to the amount they will earn during the current leave year. If your agency allows advance annual leave, you will be able to approve such requests if they do not present a staffing or workload problem for your work unit.

Even if your agency allows advance annual leave, you should carefully consider the circumstances of the request before granting it. For example, is the employee likely to return to work? Has the employee been on the rolls long enough to justify granting advance leave? If approving the advance leave does not appear to be in the best interest of the agency, you should deny the request.

Before granting *any* annual leave, you should always know whether the employee has sufficient leave "on the books" to cover the time off.

Workload does not permit approval

Sometimes your unit's workload may be too heavy, or your staff too thin to allow you to approve a leave request for a particular period. If that is the case you are entirely within your rights in turning down the request. In such situations it is a good idea to explain your reasons for denying a leave request to the employees involved, and to tell them when you expect to be able to approve leave.

Illness during scheduled annual leave.

Sometimes employees become ill or are injured while on annual leave. If such illness or injury would have incapacitated them for duty, you may retroactively approve the use of sick leave for the time they were sick or injured. Depending on your agency's rules and the circumstances, it may be a good idea to ask the employee for supporting evidence—such as a doctor's certificate—specifying the nature and period of time of the problem.

More requests than can be granted

It is common to find that many employees want to take annual leave during certain "high demand" times, such as the holiday season and the traditional summer vacation season. Often it is not possible to grant all the requests without leaving the unit under-staffed. Most agencies have established policies or labor agreement provisions that outline how procedures for determining which employees get first choice.

If there is not a formal, written procedure, there may be an unwritten practice, such as first come, first served—or most senior employees get first choice. It is important that you follow the established rules in either case, since an inconsistent approach will quickly anger employees and open you to charges of favoritism.

Case Situation

Two employees want the same week off, but you need to have at least one of them present to deal with expected workload. The employee who has been in the group longest got first choice last year, but the other employee has received an outstanding performance rating recently. Whose leave would you approve?

Answer

If the employees involved in a situation like this are unwilling or unable to work it out among themselves, you will have to decide whose request is granted. The key to handling such situations is in knowing the rules—written or unwritten—that have been used previously.

For example, if the employees are covered by a labor agreement that specifies that the most senior employee gets first choice, your decision is simple. Similarly, if an unwritten rule—usually called a "past practice"—has consistently been used in such situations in your organization, you should stick with it now. Regardless of whether you think a different rule would be better, it is a good idea to make such decisions consistent with past approaches. If you do not, employees may suspect that you are "playing favorites" or making up the rules as you go.

Annual leave and overtime in the same week

Although few agencies have policies that absolutely forbid supervisors to authorize an employee to use annual leave and work overtime on the same day or within the same week, most agencies want supervisors to avoid such situations if at all possible. If employees in your unit routinely work overtime most weeks, you may have little choice but to allow both overtime and leave within the same week. If your unit works overtime only occasionally, however, it is a good idea to avoid granting an employee annual leave during normal work hours and then having him or her work overtime. Doing so creates the appearance of poor resource management on your part.

Need to cancel previously approved annual leave

Sometimes unforeseen changes make it difficult or impossible to allow an employee to be absent during a previously-approved period. Contrary to what you may have heard, you *are* empowered to cancel leave if work requirements demand it. Because leave cancellation can be extremely unpopular with employees—and may cause serious disruption of plans or even monetary loss—it is important that you only cancel approved leave if absolutely necessary. *Do not* cancel leave as a way of administering informal discipline.

Special Leave Situations

There are several special annual leave situations you must also understand. Although they come up less often, you must know how to deal with them when they do arise. They include:

Absence for Maternity or Paternity

Agencies have established a variety of policies that deal with leave requests in connection with the birth or adoption of a child. In general, agency regulations provide that female employees may use sick leave for the period of time they are incapacitated for duty for the period of delivery and recuperation. There is no set amount of time allowed for this purpose, although many agencies routinely allow up to six weeks absence without requiring additional medical documentation.

In addition, employees are permitted to schedule annual leave or leave without pay (LWOP) to provide a reasonable time away from work in which to adjust to the arrival of a child. Employees are usually not permitted to alternate periods of annual leave and LWOP to engineer entitlement to holiday pay. Most agencies will allow employees to alternate annual leave and LWOP to moderate their income flow in such situations, however.

Finally, it is always a good idea to encourage an employee who expects to be absent for maternity purposes to schedule a sufficient amount of annual leave to avoid "use or lose" problems if she will not return before the end of the leave year.

Although male employees are not entitled to use sick leave in connection with the birth or adoption of a child, they are allowed to schedule blocks of annual leave or LWOP just as female employees are.

In dealing with leave requests for maternity or paternity reasons, it is important that you understand what you can and cannot do.

You can:

▲ Require employees to submit an SF-71 in advance, outlining the amount of time the employee expects to be absent.

▲ Require communication from the employee and/ or an additional SF-71 if the employee wants to schedule more time off.

▲ Disapprove requests for advance annual leave or extended LWOP beyond reasonable time frames if doing so would create a work load problem in your unit. In such situations, it is usually a good idea to confer with your agency's personnel specialists before disapproving a leave request.

You cannot:

▲ Require the employee to take annual leave, sick leave or LWOP before delivery.

▲ Question an employee as to whether she is planning to have a family or expecting a child.

▲ Terminate an employee or reassign him or her to a job with less grade, pay or promotion potential solely because of a request for or use of leave taken for maternity or paternity purposes.

Leave Sharing

Under a law passed in 1988 (Public Law 100-566), employees can voluntarily transfer earned annual leave to the account of another federal employee who has a bona fide medical emergency. There are several points you need to be aware of concerning the leave sharing program.

▲ Employees can donate unused annual leave to a another federal employee—in the same or even a different agency—only after the receiving employee has applied for and gotten approval to use shared leave.

▲ Employees cannot donate leave to an immediate supervisor under any circumstances, presumably to avoid the creation—or appearance—of undue pressure to do so.

▲ Employees can only donate leave that has already been earned, or will be earned during the current leave year.

▲ Donations are limited to no more than one-half the amount of leave an employee is expected to earn in the current leave year. This works out to no more than 52 hours for employees in the four-hour per pay period category; 80 hours for those who earn six per pay period; and a maximum of 104 hours for those in the eight-hour category.

▲ If a recipient does not use all of the leave donated in connection with the medical emergency, the unused portion is returned to donors on a pro-rated basis. For example, if you donated 25% of the total hours to an employee, and eight hours are unused, you would be re-credited with two hours annual leave.

Mandatory Annual Leave

In most circumstances supervisors cannot require employees to use annual leave. Doing so is usually considered a suspension, and employees may recover any leave they were required to use. There are some special situations in which employees can be given the choice of using annual leave, LWOP, or AWOL however.

▲ *Short-term shutdowns.* Some agencies and activities routinely schedule short shut-downs when it is not practical or feasible to continue operations, or when it is necessary to perform extensive plant maintenance activities.

For example, federal industrial facilities such as Navy shipyards usually shut down for one or two weeks over the year-end holiday season. During such periods there is no work available for most employees, and they have the choice of using annual leave or LWOP.

▲ *Either/or choices.* Supervisors may give employees the choice of using annual leave or having time recorded as AWOL in a variety of situations. For example, if an employee arrives late for work or without necessary equipment, you might give the employee the choice of requesting leave for the time involved or being carried AWOL.

Remember that you are generally *not* within your rights, in requiring an employee to take annual leave if he or she does not choose to do so.

Key Points:

▲ Managing annual leave is a frequent and important duty of every federal supervisor.

▲ Employees earn annual leave as a legal benefit, and are entitled to use it for recreational purposes and for the conduct of personal business.

▲ Supervisors retain the right to determine when annual leave may be used. Accordingly, employees are required to request leave—usually in advance—and are not entitled to take leave if the request is denied.

▲ Supervisors are responsible for assuring that employees schedule sufficient amounts of leave to avoid "use or lose" problems, but must also balance leave use to maintain operating efficiency within the work unit.

▲ Agencies have different rules that specify how employees may schedule leave, how preferences should be granted in setting leave schedules, how much leave may be used in each increment, whether advance leave can be scheduled, and the like. Supervisors must know and apply such rules correctly or risk the creation of unnecessary problems and complaints.

▲ Every supervisor can expect to face a variety of common leave problem situations, ranging from failure to schedule leave in advance to unexpected illness while on annual leave. It is important that you understand how to deal with such situations.

▲ Special leave situations, such as leave for maternity/paternity purposes, leave sharing and mandatory leave, operate within special rules. Before making a snap decision on such matters, it is helpful to review the rules that govern them and to discuss the situation with your servicing personnel specialist.

CHAPTER
TWO

DEALING WITH
TARDINESS AND
ATTENDANCE
PROBLEMS

CHAPTER

TWO

Dealing With Tardiness And Attendance Problems

Introduction

The single most common problem supervisors deal with, both in the federal service and in private industry, is attendance. Supervisors everywhere run into the problems of late arrivals at work (tardiness), long lunch hours, early departures, and outright failures to show up for work at all (AWOL).

In this chapter we will look into these problems and, more importantly, discuss what you can do to deal with them effectively. We will look at a related problem area, sick leave abuse, in Chapter Three.

Dealing With Tardiness

Attendance problems come in all different shapes and sizes. At the low end of the scale is the occasional situation in which a usually reliable employee oversleeps or has car trouble, and as a result arrives late for work. Regardless of whether the late arrival may be inconvenient or cause you a problem, most supervisors realize that such things happen, and often excuse such absences without any charge to leave. It is, of course, within your authority to excuse occasional short absences where you feel it is justified to do so under the circumstances.

More of a problem is the employee who often comes to work late. Regardless of whether the employee has an excuse for every late arrival, chronic tardiness can become a serious problem in any of several ways. It can irritate other employees or encourage them to drift in late as well; it can reduce both the employee's and the work group's productivity; and finally, it can establish a pattern or practice that will make it difficult for you or other supervisors to apply corrective disciplinary action in dealing with other attendance problems.

In deciding how to deal with employees who arrive late for work frequently, you need to bear in mind two key points:

▲ Regardless of how many excuses an employee may have or how valid they may sound, it is the *employee's* responsibility to get to work on time. It is up to the employee—*not you*—to solve transportation or alarm clock problems.

▲ You have the right to insist that employees report for work on time, and if they fail to do so, to take corrective action.

Requiring employees to come to work on time is neither unfair nor unreasonable, since they are paid for a whole day's work and are expected to be present during established work hours.

Taking Action

The main question, obviously, is what can you do to head off or correct a chronic tardiness problem? The answer, fortunately, is quite a bit.

An Organized Approach

The first step to avoiding or correcting attendance problems is to make sure that all of the employees who work under your direction understand clearly what your policy is regarding attendance. This does not require a major speech or lengthy written policy statement from you. All you need do is briefly outline your expectations to employees in plain English. For example:

"Since I'm fairly new to this unit (or "since we seem to be having some problems lately") I want to spell out my policy on attendance. As you know, work hours are ___ to ___. I take that seriously, and expect that all of us will be here during those hours. That means arriving on time, sticking around until the day is over, and keeping breaks and the lunch period within the established limits."

"I realize that everyone runs into a problem once in awhile, and I'm perfectly willing to grant annual leave or even administrative excusal for the occasional late arrival. But I am not willing to put up with frequent late arrivals, long lunches or early departures. If necessary I will take corrective steps if I see any of those things happening."

Keeping An Eye On Things

The next step is staying in touch with what is happening in your work unit. This does not mean standing by the door at starting and quitting times with a watch in your hand and a frown on your face. But it does mean making an effort to stay reasonably aware of whether the people you supervise are following the rules.

Spotting Problems

Tardiness problems are usually not hard to spot. Usually they involve one or two employees who arrive late fairly often, or an entire group of employees who seem to completely ignore the established work hours. In most cases, the problem involves only one or two employees. But in either case, it is up to you to note what is happening and to take corrective steps.

Getting Things Back On Track

If the problem involves only one or two employees, the best approach is to meet with them privately, one at a time, and provide specific counselling on the problem. That involves making a few simple points:

▲ Point out the established work hours and your expectation that they will appear for work on time.

▲ Briefly outline what you have observed or learned of the employee's late arrivals—giving specific information—and stress that the behavior (tardiness) is unacceptable.

▲ Ask if there is a general reason for the tardiness, and if so, point out the availability of the employee assistance program (EAP) to provide additional help and advice.

▲ Regardless of reasons or excuses, clearly state that the employee is expected to solve transportation or other problems himself or herself and to report for work on time.

▲ Stress that additional late arrivals will lead to corrective action, including discipline if necessary.

If your organization works under a flexible work hours arrangement, you may also have the ability to work with an employee to adjust starting and quitting times enough to overcome the problem. If you do not have that tool available, however, it will be necessary for the employee to find a way to correct the problem.

Case Situation

When you recently became the supervisor of a group of employees it soon became clear to you that almost everyone in the group comes in late, and that employees frequently leave early to take care of personal business or to "get a jump on the traffic." You have learned that the previous supervisor allowed this approach for several years, and the employees now regard it as a "past practice." What, if anything, can you do?

Answer

Contrary to what many supervisors and employees believe, a pattern of behavior that is directly contrary to established rules or regulations—such as the requirement to work during regular hours—does not replace a rule or stop you from enforcing it. Even if a pattern of allowing employees to arrive late and leave early has been allowed by management, you can get things back on track by clearly reminding employees of the the required starting and quitting time, and telling them you intend to enforce the rule—with discipline, if necessary.

In some situations, there may be unique circumstances where a past practice may exist. If you have any doubts or questions, it is best to check with your labor relations or personnel advisor before taking action.

Dealing With Excuses

An employee who is counseled regarding attendance problems may offer any of a variety of excuses or defenses for frequent tardiness. Several of the most common ones are listed below.

"I'm not late that often/I was only a few minutes late."

It is up to you, the supervisor, to determine whether an absence is an isolated event or a routine matter. If *you* feel the employee's late arrivals are frequent enough to create a problem, it does not matter whether the employee views her late tardiness as minor. Similarly, it is up to you to determine whether being a few minutes is acceptable.

"My car keeps breaking down/My ride is always late."

Again, these are problems for the employee to solve, not you. Although you may make suggestions and try to help the employee to identify possible solutions, ultimately it is up to the employee to get the car repaired, find a more reliable ride, or take an earlier bus. If he or she cannot solve the problem or make necessary adjustments to get to work on time, further corrective action will become appropriate.

"Other people come in late all the time and you don't give them a hard time."

Hopefully this is not true. Your best bet in dealing with this kind of assertion is to ask the employee which other employees come in late. If there is truth to the employee's claim, correct that problem as well. Without facts to back it up, this is a weak excuse. But if it is true, you should not take action against one employee until you begin enforcing the same rules for all employees.

" I get as much done as other people / Besides, I work late sometimes and it all balances out.'"

The point is that you—not the employee—are responsible for setting work hours. It is not a good idea to let everyone in the work unit to make up their own hours on a day-to-day basis.

Although it is true that most supervisors allow some slack for employees who are occasionally late—perhaps letting them "make-up" the time at the end of the day—this is not a good approach with an employee who is frequently late. Taken to an extreme, eventually the employee is setting the work hours, and you wind up with no real idea of whether it is "all evening out" or not.

Leaving A Paper Trail

Finally, it is usually a good idea to create a record of any counselling session you hold with an employee about attendance problems. The record need not be a major, formal document. A simple handwritten memo in your notebook or a note to the employee's informal file will be plenty. Informal notes of this nature are perfectly legitimate, and do not constitute discipline.

If you prefer a slightly more formal document, you might draft a memo for the record and provide a copy to the employee, or even write a short letter to the employee outlining the main points of the discussion. Samples of a typical memo for the record and letter to the employee are included at the end of this chapter.

When creating such written records, however, be sure to mention the fact to the employee and show him what you have written. Doing so will avoid any later misunderstandings or claims that you have improperly kept "secret" records.

What Next?

In most cases, once you have clearly communicated your expectations to an employee you will find that the problem disappears. If it does not, or if it temporarily stops but reappears after awhile, it will be necessary to take more formal steps to deal with the problem. Here's how to go about it.

Disapproving Annual Leave Requests

If an employee continues to come in late despite your counselling, you will want to take several follow-up steps. The first is to stop approving the use of annual leave or LWOP to cover the amount of time the employee is late.

For example, if an employee comes in 30 minutes late normally you would probably either grant administrative excusal (that is, not require the employee to use any leave) or allow the employee to take annual leave to cover the missed work time.

If an employee is frequently tardy and you are trying to correct the problem, however, it is important not to grant leave for the period of time he or she is late. Why? A labor arbitrator or the Merit Systems Protection Board (MSPB) may later rule that you approved the absence, as indicated by the grant of annual leave. In short, if you grant annual leave time to cover instances of tardiness, they may not count as infractions in later trying to take disciplinary action because the employee's absence was approved—as indicated by the grant of annual leave.

So what should you do? Record the employee as being AWOL—or on "unexcused absence"—for the amount of time he is late. As a result, the employee will not be paid for that amount of time, and you will have created an official record of unapproved, unexcused tardiness in that instance.

Letter of Warning

Depending on the circumstances, at this point you may also want to take the first step toward formal disciplinary action. In most agencies that requires that you provide the employee a formal letter of warning, which is just what it sound like. Although most agencies do not consider such letters to be actual discipline, they do provide a formal caution to the employee that further tardiness will result in discipline. Because agencies use different formats in such letters, you should always consult with your agency's personnel or employee relations specialists for help in drafting one.

Disciplinary Action

Fortunately, by the time you reach the letter of warning stage, the overwhelming majority of employees have long since decided it is time to follow the rules. Unfortunately, however, a few may continue to ignore warnings. What then?

If the problem continues after a formal warning, it is time to begin formal disciplinary action. In most agencies that would mean at least a Letter of Reprimand for the next instance of tardiness. Such letters are considered discipline, and they usually remain in employees' official personnel folders for a period of 1-3 years. More importantly, they provide a first step on the road to progressively tougher disciplinary action if the employee does not correct her behavior.

In the rare cases in which such lower-level discipline is not sufficient to turn things around, progressively longer suspensions without pay can be used for further infractions. And ultimately, employees can—and have been—permanently removed for chronic tardiness.

For example, in a recently reported case the MSPB upheld the removal of an employee for chronic tardiness when the total work time the employee had missed amounted to less than eight hours! In approving the termination, the Board noted that the agency had applied progressively stronger disciplinary actions, but the employee had persisted in coming to work late.

The Bottom Line

The point of all this is not to encourage you to discipline employees at the drop of a hat—or at the first instance of late arrival. You need to exercise judgment and recognize when you have a problem that requires corrective steps, and when you are dealing with the routine, occasional late arrival problems that everyone experiences from time to time.

The most important point to remember is that you have the responsibility and authority to deal with problems when you identify them. Attendance is a serious matter, and poor attendance habits are disruptive. The bottom line is, when all is said and done, you are in charge and must take the steps necessary to deal with such problems when they crop up.

Other Problems Managing Annual Leave

Although the most frequent problems supervisors face in connection with annual leave involve tardiness, other problems also crop up occasionally.

Calling-In

Most organizations establish specific call-in procedures for employees to request annual or sick leave on short notice. The rules covering such situations might be found in agency regulations, a shop standard operating procedure (SOP), or in the labor agreement covering bargaining unit employees.

Although the rules vary from one organization to another, they generally require that employees who have not already obtained permission to be absent must call-in before or shortly after the start of the workday to request leave. Some units require that such calls must go to an employee's immediate supervisor, while others allow employees to contact almost anyone in supervision or administration.

Problems arise when employees either do not call-in at all when absent for a day or do not call the designated person to obtain approval of a leave request. A similar problem is that of having someone else call-in for them.

Failure to Call-In

The most serious problem involving call-ins is the outright failure to contact the agency at all to explain an unscheduled absence from work. Obviously an unplanned, unannounced absence can be extremely disruptive, particularly if the employee is part of a work team.

Rarely, if ever, should such absences be allowed to pass without disciplinary action unless the employee provides sufficient evidence of an emergency situation that:

a) Prevented him from coming to work, and

b) Prevented him from calling-in to notify you.

Absent such evidence, it is usually appropriate to carry the employee as AWOL for the time away from work, and also to recommend or start formal disciplinary action. Discussion with your agency's personnel specialists will help you determine the appropriate penalty to apply in a particular situation.

Calling Someone Else

If an employee feels that you are unlikely to approve a sudden annual leave request, she may attempt to duck the problem by calling-in to a secretary or other supervisor.

If you have an established rule that requires the employee to call you directly, or if you have previously told the employee that all annual leave requests must go directly to you, again you would be within your rights in marking the time absent as AWOL, and possibly using disciplinary action.

Before taking such steps, however, make certain that you have communicated your requirements to the employee very clearly, and that your directions are in line with agency or labor agreement rules.

Although you may not require other employees to request leave from you directly, it still may be proper to place that requirement on a particular employee with an established record of last-minute, inconvenient leave requests. You should talk to your personnel or labor relations specialist before singling a particular employee out for such a requirement.

Someone Else Calling

A close cousin of the misdirected call-in is having another person phone in to state that so-and-so is taking leave. Absent a very good reason—(the employee is in jail and used his only call to round-up a lawyer)—this is usually not acceptable. You may take the same steps outlined above in dealing with such problems. That is, you can disapprove the leave request, inform the caller the employee is to report for work immediately, and carry the employee as AWOL for any missed time.

Key Points

▲ Tardiness is the most common attendance problem supervisors face.

▲ Supervisors are entitled to use judgment in determining whether tardiness is occasional and therefore excusable, or part of a pattern that requires correction. It is extremely important to be fair and consistent in handling such matters, however.

▲ You bear primary responsibility for spotting and correcting attendance problems.

▲ Although routine counselling is effective in correcting most attendance problems, you may find it necessary to use formal warnings or even disciplinary action to correct chronic attendance problems in some cases.

▲ In dealing with employee excuses or defenses for chronic attendance problems it is important to recognize that the employee "owns" the problem, and is directly responsible for solving it.

▲ Unexcused absences from work should be charged to AWOL, not annual leave, if you wish to reflect that the absence was not approved.

▲ Agency call-in rules are important and can be enforced through the use of discipline, if necessary.

APPENDIX A:

Sample Memorandum for the Record

To: File   Date

From: Your name

Subject: Attendance Counselling [Employee's Name]

On [date], [employee name] did not report to work at the scheduled time; nor did [he/she] call in to request leave or to report the reasons for [his/her] absence.

[He/she] reported to work the next day at the normal time. [He/she] stated that the reason for absence on [date] was that a dependent child was ill and [he/she] had to stay home to care for the child. When asked why the employee did not call in, [he/she] stated that the phone was out of order.

I reminded the employee that [he/she] is always required to call-in to request leave unless absolutely unable to do so. In this situation it may have been possible to phone in from a neighbor's telephone or to use a nearby pay phone.

I have also advised Mr./Ms. [name] that failing to call-in when absent from scheduled work without a sufficient reason will lead to discipline in the future.

Appendix B:

Sample Counselling Letter

To: Employee Name   Date

From: Your Name

Subject: Tardiness Counselling Meeting

On [date] I met with you to discuss your late arrival at work on several recent occasions [include dates if available]. At our meeting I provided you a copy of the rules governing attendance and explained the office policy on tardiness to you. I also pointed out that tardiness is unacceptable in this organization, and that further incidents can and will lead to disciplinary action.

You noted that you have had problems starting your car, and that it sometimes takes more time than expected to drop your child off at the child care center. Although I recognize that such problems can occur, I pointed out that you will have to resolve such issues yourself and report to work on time.

This letter is to confirm our discussion in writing and to remind you that:

1. It is your responsibility to arrive at work on time each day.

2. I consider your tardiness a very serious matter and unacceptable behavior.

3. Future instances of tardiness may result in disciplinary action, up to and including removal from the federal service.

4. If you have any personal problems that may be affecting your ability to report to duty on time, you may seek the assistance of the Employee Assistance Program by calling [phone number].

Appendix C

Guidelines For Conducting Attendance Counselling Meetings

Attendance counselling should be conducted in a private setting, where your words will not be overheard by other employees. You can expect better results from such a meeting if you plan it in advance, and have specific objectives. The following list highlights the key points you should bear in mind in planning a counselling session.

▲ Clearly tell the employee what the problem is; for example, coming to work late, leaving early, lengthy lunches, or failing to call-in or schedule leave in advance.

▲ Explain the the applicable leave and attendance rules in your organization, and your specific requirements—such as calling in directly to you for approval of annual leave.

▲ Ask the employee if there is a general reason for her attendance problems. If there is and the reason relates to a personal problem (family problems, alcohol or drug abuse etc.), refer the employee to the Employee Assistance Program.

▲ Clearly state that attendance is a serious matter, and that further infractions will lead to disciplinary action.

▲ Make sure the employee knows that you consider this to be her problem, not yours, and that she is responsible for correcting it.

▲ If appropriate, tell the employee that you will be following up the meeting with a letter confirming the discussion or making some other written record of the conversation. If the employee requests, allow him or her to review your written notes or memorandum of the meeting.

CHAPTER
THREE

MANAGING SICK
LEAVE

CHAPTER THREE

Managing Sick Leave

Introduction

With the possible exception of annual leave, sick leave raises more questions and provides more problems for supervisors than any other type of leave. That is somewhat surprising, since the rules governing sick leave are generally more simple and straightforward than those governing annual leave. But employees sometimes misuse sick leave, and supervisors often are unsure of how to handle the issues that come up.

In this chapter we will look into the basic information you need to know about sick leave, examine the kinds of problems that often come up, and spell out your role in managing sick leave effectively.

Basic Principles

Employees earn sick leave and are entitled to use it for specific purposes that are outlined under applicable law and regulations. In general, employees are entitled to use sick leave when they are incapacitated for duty by illness or injury, or are caring for a relative who is suffering from a contagious disease. In addition, employees are eligible to use sick leave to receive medical, dental or optical treatment or examination with supervisory approval.

Employees earn sick leave at different rates, depending on the number of hours they work. Full-time employees earn four hours sick leave per pay period. Part-time employees earn sick leave on a pro-rated basis linked to the number of hours the employee works each pay period. Unlike annual leave, employees may accumulate an unlimited amount of sick leave and are encouraged to do so.

Although employees earn sick leave as a benefit established in law and are entitled to use it for specified purposes, its use is subject to approval by agency managers and supervisors. In short, management officials are responsible for making certain that sick leave is being used correctly, and may disapprove sick leave requests that do not meet requirements.

Rules Governing Sick Leave

The rules governing sick leave are also fairly simple, although they vary somewhat from one agency to another. The main issues that you need to understand are listed below.

Request and Approval Procedures

Employees are not free to take sick leave whenever they feel it appropriate to do so. Like annual leave, sick leave must be requested and approved. That usually means that an employee who is ill or injured must contact his supervisor either before or shortly after the beginning of a scheduled workday, inform her of the problem and request leave. Some agencies also require employees to submit leave request forms (SF-71) for all instances of sick leave.

Although sick leave may be approved retroactively for legitimate purposes, it may be appropriate to counsel or discipline an employee if he or she did not follow established sick leave request procedures.

Allowable Purposes

As noted above, sick leave can be used when an employee is incapacitated for work (that is, unable to perform) as a result of illness or injury, or an employee is caring for someone with a contagious disease.

These first two situations give supervisors no alternative but to approve the leave. If, indeed, an employee is genuinely unable to work because of illness or injury, or is caring for a person with a contagious disease, she has the right under law to use earned sick leave.

If an employee is *not* truly incapacitated for duty, of course, you can—and should—disapprove sick leave. To cite an extreme example, if an employee called in sick with a hangnail on a toe, it would be reasonable to consider that person not completely incapacitated for work. At the very least, the employee ought to be capable of light duty work at a desk.

You may recall that employees also can use sick leave to attend a medical, dental or optical treatment or examination. You may disapprove requests to use sick leave for voluntary activities such as pre-scheduled examinations, however, if the employee's absence would interfere with the operation of the work unit. As a matter of fact, many agencies' leave regulations strongly encourage employees to schedule such routine appointments outside of work hours if at all possible.

Note, however, that if the prevailing practice in your organization is to grant sick leave for routine medical appointments, you should not flatly disapprove such requests without talking with your agency's personnel or labor relations specialists.

Advance Sick Leave Requests

Employees may be granted up to 30 days advance sick leave in connection with a serious illness, injury or disability if the employee has exhausted his or her sick leave balance and expects to continue employment with the agency following recovery. This is a sort of "loan" of sick leave that the employee must later "pay back" by earning the amount of leave used.

Policies on granting advance sick leave vary from agency to agency, so you should check your agency's requirements before approving a request for advance sick leave. In addition, advance sick leave usually requires several levels of supervisory approval under most agencies' rules.

Requirements for Supporting Evidence

Because agency managers and supervisors are responsible for making certain that sick leave is used appropriately, you are entitled to require supporting evidence of illness, injury, or treatment in some circumstances. This might include a signed notice ("medical certificate") from a medical practitioner or other corroborating information, such as a dated prescription container.

Most agencies require such supporting evidence only in cases of extended absence (usually three days or more); or if an employee is suspected of regular sick leave abuse and has been placed on a requirement to support all sick leave usage with a medical certificate; or if the circumstances of the employee's request raise reasonable suspicions in your mind.

Common Sick Leave Problems

The problems supervisors have in administering and controlling sick leave use tend to fall into a handful of categories.

Routine Sick Leave Abuse

This refers to the situation in which an employee uses sick leave to supplement his or her annual leave fairly often. Indeed, the employee may view sick leave as an absolute entitlement to time off, regardless of whether he is ill or not.

You can spot routine sick leave abuse by looking for any of several things:

▲ Regular patterns of use

The key to spotting patterns is to see if sick leave is used frequently in connection with certain events. For example, on Mondays, Fridays or before or after holidays. Or, perhaps the day after a scheduled activity, such as a weeknight night bowling league.

▲ Chronically low sick leave balance

If an employee has not suffered a major illness or injury but has little or no sick leave built up, it could be that the employee is merely frail and sickly. More often, however, it means that the employee has been regularly using sick leave as a way to get time off.

▲ Announced or indicated by events

Some employees virtually announce when they are going to take sick leave inappropriately. You may have seen situations in which employees stated they "planned to get sick" to avoid a particular work assignment, to go hunting or fishing or to attend a wedding or class reunion.

Suspicious Sick Leave Requests

Although perhaps not "pattern" sick leave abusers, some employees request leave in circumstances that make it fairly clear that they are not actually ill.

For example, an employee is confronted with an undesirable work assignment, unwanted overtime or some other unpleasant event and immediately announces that he or she is sick. Or an employee requests annual leave and is turned down because of work load demands, but calls in sick on the requested days off. Or an employee calls in after his or her shift has already started and requests sick leave with the sounds of a party going on in the background.

In any of these situations (all drawn from actual cases), you might reasonably suspect intended sick leave abuse.

Failure to Call-In or Keep Supervision Notified of Status

Another common problem is an outright failure to call in to request sick leave during the work day. In such situations an employee may "retroactively" request sick leave after he or she has returned to work. Similarly, an employee may call in sick one day, but remain absent for several more with no further attempt to communicate with you. In such cases it is usually appropriate to counsel employees concerning sick leave request rules, and/or to initiate disciplinary action for failure to follow established request procedures.

Supervisor's Responsibility and Authority

As a supervisor, it is your responsibility to respond to all requests for sick leave. If a request appears valid and you do not suspect sick leave abuse, your job is easy: Approve the request.

But what if you suspect that an employee is not genuinely ill or injured? What can you do then— especially since, as some employees like to point out, you are probably not a doctor? Let's look at each of the problem situations we identified above in answering that question.

Handling Pattern Sick Leave Abuse

In many ways pattern sick leave abuse is the easiest situation to handle. Here's why.

Your role in dealing with this type of problem is simply to spot the apparent pattern, counsel the employee, and if the problem continues, place the employee on what is usually called a *"letter of requirement"* or on a *"sick leave restriction list."*

In counseling an employee who appears to be developing a sick leave abuse pattern you should stress several things:

▲ Your concern about possible abuse;

▲ The importance of building and maintaining a reserve of sick leave hours for use in the event of serious injury or long-term illness;

▲ The consequences of sick leave abuse, including being placed on a sick leave restriction status, and possible discipline.

Once placed under a letter of requirement or sick leave restriction status or whatever your agency may call it, an employee must obtain a medical certificate from a medical practitioner to support every sick leave request he makes. Obviously, that can be inconvenient, to say nothing of expensive. For that reason, putting this requirement on employees tends to discourage pattern sick leave abuse. If the employee continues to abuse sick leave, of course, you may have to resort to disciplinary steps.

Before using a sick leave restriction letter, however, you also need to be aware that each agency has its own rules for handling such situations. For example, your agency may require that you provide a specific, written warning to an employee first. Or it may limit the amount of time you can keep an employee under such a restriction to a specific period, such as six months or a year. In addition, labor agreements might require that you review the employee's sick leave record after some period of time and release the restriction if no further abuse has occurred.

Despite such procedural issues, however, the fact remains that the sick leave restriction letter is a powerful tool you can use to discourage pattern sick leave abuse.

Handling Suspicious Sick Leave Requests

This category of problems is somewhat more difficult to deal with, but you have considerably more control than many supervisors think.

As noted above, suspicious requests are those that come up in situations that could cause a reasonable person to question whether the employee is actually ill or injured. For example, after trying to get out of an overtime assignment an employee suddenly announces that he or she is ill, and wants to take sick leave.

As employees often point out, supervisors are not usually doctors, and therefore are not medically qualified to determine whether the employee is, in fact, ill or injured. Therefore, employees often contend, you have no choice but to grant the sick leave request.

Fortunately, in most agencies that is not the case. Granted, you are probably *not* a doctor and therefore not capable of rendering valid medical opinions. But you *are* capable of determining when a sick leave request is suspicious under the circumstances or appears to fall short of a valid reason to be absent from work.

If you have reason to believe an employee is not genuinely entitled to sick leave, under most agencies' regulations and even under most labor agreements, you are entitled to hold off granting sick leave—or to grant it "conditionally"—until the employee produces acceptable supporting evidence of illness or injury. (In other words, until the employee produces a medical certificate from a doctor).

Dealing With Suspicious Medical Evidence

In some situations, you may be entitled to require additional information to support a sick leave request. For example, a supervisor at one agency noticed that a particular employee routinely announced that he had a doctor's appointment for the treatment of a back injury whenever he was tapped for an unwelcome overtime assignment. Although he invariably returned with a certificate from the doctor's office, the supervisor noticed that the slips had only a stamped signature, with only the date written in.

When the employee was told to produce a written, signed note from the doctor, he refused to comply. Further investigation revealed that the employee had taken a pad of excuse slips from the receptionist's desk, and was simply filling in the date himself whenever he wanted to be off work.

What's the point? Simply that you are entitled to reasonable evidence that an employee actually qualifies for sick leave before granting a request. If you have reasonable doubts, do not hesitate to ask for additional proof.

Note, however, that some agencies have agreed to labor contract provisions that restrict the situations in which you can require an employee to produce a medical certificate. Be certain to check your agency's regulations and labor agreement provisions before ordering employees to bring in a doctor's slip.

Handling Failures to Call In

Sometimes employees simply fail to show up for work and do not call in to request sick leave until a day or more later. In such circumstances you must, as in the other situations, apply your own best judgment.

If the employee claims that he or she was unable to call in for some good reason, and if you find the explanation believable, you can approve sick leave for the period of absence. To cite an example, in one reported case an employee was seriously ill while on a backpacking trip in a remote area and unable to get to a telephone for several days.

On the other hand, if you find the explanation un-believable for any reason—for example, the employ-ee was too ill to call in but was later observed sing-ing with a local rock band that evening—you can disapprove the request and carry the employee as AWOL for the time away from the job. To put it simply, employees are required to follow leave re-quest procedures in obtaining sick leave as well. Failure to do so can provide a valid reason for charging AWOL or taking disciplinary action.

As a general rule, rarely should you find it neces-sary to retroactively grant sick leave to an employ-ee who has failed to show up for work, did not call in, and has not produced other convincing evidence of serious incapacitation that also prevented him or her from contacting you.

Special Problems

There are several special situations you also need to be aware of in managing employees' sick leave.

Chronic or Long-Term Illness or Disability

Sometimes employees contract long-term illnesses or suffer disabling injuries that exhaust all sick and annual leave, without the employee recovering sufficiently to resume his or her duties.

In such situations the employee may be able to qualify for disability retirement, although it is usually up to the employee to seek it. Unfortunately, sometimes employees do not qualify for such retirement but are still unable to resume the duties of the position. In such cases, if there are no other vacant positions the employee is qualified to hold and there are no other reasonable accommodations that can be made which will allow the employee to work, the agency may have no choice but to separate the employee for disability reasons. If you find yourself facing such a situation, work closely with your agency's personnel specialists before taking any action.

Alcohol or Drug-Related Problems

Unfortunately, employees' attendance problems are sometimes linked to drug or alcohol abuse. If you have reason to suspect that an employee's overuse or abuse of sick leave is related to one of these problems, it is important that you clearly advise the employee of the agency's EAP, and recommend that he or she contact an EAP counselor for assistance.

Here are some signs to watch for in identifying possible alcohol or drug abuse related to sick leave use:

▲ Voice or speech patterns that suggest intoxication or drug influence when an employee calls to request leave. For example, slurred or incoherent speech, uncontrolled laughter, noticeably slower or faster speaking.

▲ Physical indications, such as drowsiness, bloodshot eyes, odor of alcohol, unsteadiness, and the like.

▲ Regular use of sick leave immediately after paydays or weekends.

▲ Erratic mood swings or hyperactivity, especially if they occur after brief absences from the work area.

If you are involved in taking disciplinary action based on attendance problems, it is a good idea to be sensitive to possible indications of drug or alcohol abuse. It is not up to you to diagnose a drug or alcohol problem. Nor should you try to force an admission out of an employee or force him or her into the EAP. You should, however, clearly advise such employees of the availability of the EAP if it appears there might be a problem of this nature. You should also carefully document your efforts to refer an employee for assistance.

If an employee informs you that he or she is experiencing alcohol or drug addiction problems, you will be required to cooperate in efforts to reasonably accommodate the employee's problem. That may mean, for example, that you might have to approve time off for the employee to participate in a rehabilitation program. You also may have to hold up a pending disciplinary action that you started before the employee's admission of a substance abuse problem if there is a clear connection between the misconduct and the employee's alcoholism or addiction.

But note that an employee who is involved in a drug or alcohol dependency problem is still required to follow agency rules—including those that establish leave and attendance requirements. In other words, although you are required to cooperate in reasonable efforts to help an employee to overcome a drug or alcohol problem, you *are not* obliged to tolerate continued late arrivals or failures to show up for work. If the employee does not improve his or her attendance despite reasonable accommodation efforts, discipline will be appropriate regardless of the drug or alcohol problem.

Prior to taking disciplinary action, you need to give the employee a "firm choice" between rehabilitating herself or being terminated. Carefully document your referral and counselling efforts for use later on if it becomes necessary.

Counselling Employees On Sick Leave Use

If it becomes necessary to counsel an employee regarding his or her use of sick leave, you should arrange to meet in a private setting. You should also have specific objectives and an overall plan to guide you through the meeting. The following tips will help you in preparing and conducting such counseling sessions.

▲ Explain to the employee why you believe there may be a problem by pointing out specific facts. For example, "I have noticed that you have requested sick leave on almost every Monday for the past several months, and I am not aware of any on-going health problem you might have that would explain that pattern."

▲ Discuss why you consider the facts you have mentioned to present a problem. For example, "It appears that we cannot count on having you here on Mondays, and that is very disruptive to our work plans. It is also a potentially serious problem if you should become seriously ill or injured, since you have almost no sick leave available and are using it faster than you are earning it."

▲ Ask the employee if there is a particular reason for his recent sick leave use. If the person indicates that he is suffering from a specific ailment or under a course of treatment, the use of sick leave—though extensive—might be perfectly legitimate. If, on the other hand, the illnesses are based on a miscellaneous collection of complaints, it is more likely that sick leave is being misused.

▲ Point out to the employee that the agency maintains an Employee Assistance Program, which is available to provide assistance if there is a personal or health-related problem behind the sick leave usage. Make sure the employee knows how to contact the EAP program staff and offer to schedule the appointment if that would be more comfortable for the employee. Explain to her that if she does have a problem, she will have to rehabilitate herself or face the consequences, including disciplinary action or termination.

▲ If it appears that the employee may be abusing sick leave, explain that continuing to maintain a low leave balance for suspiciously minor, miscellaneous complaints, or the development of an apparent pattern of abuse may result in a letter of requirement. Explain what that means, and that charges to AWOL and disciplinary action can result from unexcused or undocumented absences.

▲ Explain the agency policy on using sick leave only if genuinely incapacitated for duty, or for scheduled medical, dental or optical appointments.

▲ Inform the employee that you intend to follow up the counseling meeting with a memo or letter summarizing the meeting. On request, show the employee any notes you make concerning the session.

A Final Note

The key to dealing effectively with sick leave abuse problems is spotting patterns and trends that indicate possible misuse, and then providing solid counseling and advice to employees. But doing so means paying close attention—on a regular basis—to what is going on with your employees, and taking prompt steps to head off problems before they start.

Key Points

▲ Managing sick leave is one of the more challenging tasks supervisors face.

▲ Employees are entitled to use sick leave when incapacitated for duty, but supervisors are responsible for making certain that employees are using sick leave appropriately.

▲ Employees are generally required to request sick leave and receive approval from their immediate supervisor. If it appears that sick leave may not be appropriate, supervisors are entitled to seek additional supporting evidence of illness or injury.

▲ Common problems involving sick leave abuse include routine, "pattern" use of sick leave to supplement annual leave, and one-time requests for sick leave under suspicious circumstances.

▲ Supervisors can place employees who have established an apparent pattern of sick leave abuse on a "letter of requirement" or "sick leave restriction list" that forces the employee to obtain a medical certificate in support of every sick leave request. Supervisors can also require medical certificates in situations in which it appears that an employee may not actually be ill or injured.

▲ If an employee appears to have a possible drug or alcohol problem in connection with his or her leave usage, supervisors must refer the employee to the agency's employee assistance program (EAP).

▲ If an employee confirms an alcohol or drug problem, you must be willing to "reasonably accommodate" the employee in an effort to assist in his or her rehabilitation. If the employee continues to violate leave or attendance rules, however, discipline may still be imposed.

▲ The key to heading off sick leave abuse is keeping an eye on sick leave usage, spotting suspicious patterns and trends, and providing effective counseling to employees.

Appendix A: Sample Letter Of Requirement

To: Employee name   Date

From: Your name

Subject: Requirement to provide medical evidence to support sick leave requests

On [date], I met with you to discuss your use of sick leave. At that meeting I pointed out that you have used an excessive amount of sick leave in a pattern that suggests sick leave abuse. I also discussed agency rules governing the use of sick leave, and explained how to request sick leave.

Your leave pattern did not show the immediate and sustained improvement that I explained was necessary. Accordingly, this letter is to inform you that, based on the matters we discussed, effective immediately, you are required to support any use of sick leave with medical evidence of illness, injury or treatment by a physician or dentist, regardless of the length of absence from work. Such medical certification must be presented upon your return to work unless a specific extension of time is granted.

Such evidence must consist of a note, letter or memorandum completed by a licensed medical practitioner. The document must be dated and signed by the practitioner and must include:

1. The general nature of the illness, injury or treatment;

2. A statement certifying that you were unable to work due to the condition under treatment, and the specific dates of your incapacitation;

If you have medical or personal problems of any nature that may be affecting your ability to report to duty, you may seek assistance from the Employee Assistance Program by calling [phone number].

Excessive or unsubstantiated use of sick leave from this point on may result in absence-without-leave (AWOL) being charged for the time of your absence. Although not a disciplinary action, AWOL can be used as the basis for disciplinary action being taken against you.

This letter of requirement will remain in effect until [date] or until such time as you have demonstrated that you are using sick leave appropriately.

Appendix B: Potential Indications Of Sick Leave Abuse

In reviewing sick leave usage, look for frequent absences:

• *On Mondays, Fridays or the day before or after the end of the regular work week*

• *On the day before or after holidays*

• *On the day after payday*

• *On the same weekday repeatedly*

• *During hunting or fishing seasons*

• *During periods of high overtime or undesirable work assignments*

• *During a spouse or other family member's time off; for example, during school vacation periods, company shut-downs, non-federal holidays*

Also check for sick leave use that consists of:

• *Frequent absences of one or two days with no indication of an on-going health problem*

• *Numerous absences based on miscellaneous complaints unrelated to a specific injury or illness.*

CHAPTER FOUR

OTHER LEAVE CATEGORIES

Chapter Four

Other Leave Categories

Introduction

Although sick leave and annual leave are the two leave categories that most frequently require your attention, there are several other leave situations that come up from time to time.

In this chapter we will briefly introduce several additional leave categories and highlight the key points you need to know about them.

Administrative Leave (Excused Absence)

Although there is not actually a particular form or category of leave called "administrative leave" in law or OPM regulations, we all use the term and most of us have a fairly clear idea of what we mean.

Administrative leave refers to a broad variety of situations in which agency managers and supervisors are authorized to excuse employees from their normal work duties without charge to leave or loss of pay. Stated more accurately, such situations probably should be called "administrative excusals," but we will stick with the common term, administrative leave.

Administrative Leave Situations

There are a broad range of situations in which agency managers and supervisors can grant administrative leave to individuals or to groups of employees. The more common situations include:

▲ *Blood donation and recovery time*

In many agencies it is customary to allow employees up to four hours time on-the-clock in which to donate blood and recover from the effects of doing so. Note, however, that such policies normally do not guarantee a flat grant of four hours off—but only provide that up to that amount of time may be excused.

▲ *Absence or late arrival because of bad weather*

As a supervisor you are entitled to excuse an employee who arrives late because of particularly bad weather and associated traffic problems. On a larger scale, management may excuse all employees for the entire day, or allow everyone to leave early. Note that agencies are not required to convert to administrative leave the time of employees who may have been on approved annual or sick leave when such administrative excusals occur unless the agency is closed for the entire day.

85

▲ *Excusal to vote*

Many agencies and field installations—particularly those located in more remote areas—grant employees on-the-clock time to allow them to vote if polls will not be open at least three hours before or after scheduled work hours. Such time off is not simply an extension of annual leave, however. It is granted—and must be used for—the purpose of voting.

▲ *Participation in community safety or defense activities*

Agencies sometimes approve administrative leave to participate in important community efforts, such as service in a volunteer fire department.

▲ *Agency-sponsored health activities*

Many agencies now provide time during the work day to participate in "wellness" activities, including various exercise programs and attendance at health-related lectures.

▲ *Representation of employee organizations*

Agencies routinely provide considerable amounts of time for employees to represent various organizations, such as federal employee unions, on the clock. This may include not only routine duties, such as grievance handling, but also attendance at special training sessions related to the organization and its functions. Agency managers and supervisors are required to keep track of such time, and to make certain that it is being used appropriately.

▲ *Brief tardiness or absence*

As noted in the chapter on annual leave, your agency may authorize you to excuse occasional late arrivals or brief absences of up to one hour where appropriate.

Leave Without Pay (LWOP)

This is just what it sounds like—approved absence from work, but without either pay or charge to annual leave. There are several things to keep in mind concerning LWOP:

▲ LWOP is voluntary

In other words, you cannot place an employee on LWOP unless he or she requests that you do so. You cannot place an employee on LWOP as a disciplinary penalty or require an employee to request it.

▲ *Employees are not legally entitled to LWOP*

This means that the determination of whether to approve a request for LWOP is entirely up to agency management. Unlike annual and sick leave, this is not a benefit granted to employees by law, but rather, a privilege management can choose to extend on a case-by-case basis.

An exception to this is that veterans are entitled to annual leave or leave without pay for scheduled treatment of problems created while in military service. Also, an employee who is in the military reserves is entitled to leave without pay to attend reserve duty if military leave is exhausted.

▲ *There is no legal limit on the amount of LWOP that can be approved*

In most cases LWOP is approved for relatively brief periods of time, although it is sometimes granted to allow an employee to participate in an extended course of instruction or serve as a union representative on a full-time basis.

▲ *LWOP is often used in the following situations:*

• An employee has exhausted earned leave and has a legitimate need for additional time off.

• An employee wishes to participate in a project, educational experience or other matter that will require lengthy absence from the job.

• An employee requires additional time off to recover from illness or disability that is not permanently disqualifying.

▲ *You should avoid approving LWOP when:*

• You cannot excuse the employee from work without creating a staffing problem.

• An employee has not properly requested LWOP in advance for sound purposes.

• An employee is seeking to use LWOP to supplement annual leave inappropriately.

Court Leave

Court leave is an excusal from duty without loss of pay or charge to annual leave to serve as a witness or perform jury duty in a federal, state, county or municipal court. A military court is considered the same as a federal court. Accordingly, an employee may be granted court leave to serve as a witness, for example, in a military court martial.

If an employee is called to serve as a witness for the U.S. or a state or local government in his official capacity, however, court leave is not applicable. In these situations the employee is performing an official duty.

For example, if an official of the FAA were called as a witness in a state court proceeding regarding the safety features of a proposed airport, she would be present as an official duty, not on court leave. If the same employee were testifying purely as an interested local citizen, however, she would be eligible for court leave if either the U.S. or a state or local government is a party to the suit..

Employees may also qualify for court leave if serving as a witness on behalf of a private party if either the U.S. or a state or local government is a party to the suit.

Employees are not eligible for court leave, however, to serve as a witness on behalf of a private party that does not involve the federal , state or local governments, and the employee is not testifying in an official capacity. For example, if you were called by a plaintiff to testify about a traffic accident you saw while on the way to work, you would not qualify for court leave.

Permanent or temporary employees with a regularly scheduled tours of duty are eligible for court leave. Court leave is granted only for absence during hours the employee would otherwise be in a pay status. An employee cannot be granted court leave for jury or witness duty performed within a period of nonpay status. For example, if an employee were called to jury duty while on an extended period of LWOP, he or she would not be eligible for court leave. Employees who are on call for jury duty but who are excused from serving during a work day are expected to return to work.

Military Leave

Military leave is about what you might expect also. It is the approved absence from duty to perform military duty or to participate in required military reserve training without loss of pay—including normal overtime earnings—or charge to annual leave. An eligible employee can earn a maximum of 15 days of military leave per calendar year that can be used when he or she is ordered to active duty. If not used, up to 15 days military leave can be carried forward for use in another year.

Military leave is available only to employees whose appointment is for more than one year. An employee appointed on a "when-actually-employed" basis is not eligible for military leave. Employees normally must present official orders to verify their performance of military duty.

If the employee volunteers for the military duty, rather than being ordered to duty, he is still entitled to military leave once he presents his orders to the supervisor.

Home Leave

Home leave is a benefit extended to civilian employees who serve in a variety of posts located outside the continental U.S. It is earned and credited on a monthly basis. Eligible employees who agree in writing to serve an additional tour of duty at the same or another overseas post may be granted home leave after completion of a basic period of 24 months of continuous service.

Employees who return to the United States for vacation purposes are generally required to use accrued home leave before using accrued annual leave, unless the annual leave would be forfeited.

If an employee does not return to service abroad after using home leave, he or she will owe the agency that amount of leave.

Family Leave

Federal employee are now eligible for *family leave.* Family leave entitles an employee to be absent from the job for up to 12 weeks during any 12-month period. The employee does not receive any pay for the period of absence.

Family leave may be granted for a variety of events such as:

- birth and care of a child;

- adopting a child or assuming foster care for a child;

- caring for a family member with a serious health condition;

- a serious health problem which makes an employee unable to perform his job.

While on family leave, an employee may maintain health benefits coverage. It is the employee's responsibility to pay his share of health benefit costs; however, payment can be made while the employee is absent or when he returns to work.

When the employee returns, the agency must return her to the same job she left or to an equivalent job. In other words, the agency does not have to keep the same job open while the employee is absent on family leave; it only has to guarantee the employee she will get one that is substantially the same upon returning to work.

Using "Official Time"

"Official time" is not leave in the usual sense. The phrase refers to the time spent by a union official who spends time working for a union that represents Federal employees while still being paid by the agency.

As a supervisor or manager responsible for accomplishing the work of your organization, your primary concern may not be why an employee is absent; rather, you are probably more concerned that they are not available for work. As the focus of this book is to help you manage more effectively, we have included a discussion of "official time" as part of this book.

The labor relations law governing federal employees states that a union representative is entitled to receive official time to engage in *representational activities* in any amount the agency and the union agree to be "reasonable, necessary, and in the public interest." The first question you may have is, "What are representational activities?" In general, they include efforts on behalf of bargaining unit employees, such as investigating or presenting grievances, meeting with managers, or serving on joint safety committees.

For more information on the labor relations rights and responsibilities of a Federal supervisor, see *The Supervisor's Guide to Federal Labor Relations* (2nd Edition), ©1993 by FPMI Communications, Inc., Huntsville, AL

Although union officials may negotiate a collective bargaining agreement with the agency, a federal supervisor is most likely to be affected by requests for time to engage in other representational activities—such as handling an employee's grievance or discussing a problem with working conditions.

What's Not Covered

A representative is *not* entitled to use official time to carry out *internal union* business. This generally includes such things as soliciting new members, working on a union newsletter, election of union representatives, or collection of dues.

Any internal union business must be conducted on the representative's own time, such as before or after work, while on annual leave, or during a lunch break.

Read Your Agreement

Granting or denying official time is a contract administration decision. The first step you should take is to carefully read the applicable portions of the labor contract applicable to the union representative under your supervision to see how it applies to a representative's request for time. In some cases, your contract will establish guidelines for granting or denying the amount of time that can be used. If that is the case, your job will be straightforward—you only need to determine whether the amount of time requested falls within the constraints in the agreement. In many agreements, however, you will find that the contract only says that a representative is entitled to "reasonable time."

In interpreting and applying "reasonable" you will want to check with your labor relations advisor to determine the past practice of your organization, whether any grievance or arbitration decisions have been issued on the subject in your organization, and whether there is any bargaining history that will shed some light on how to handle your specific problem. You should also become familiar with any internal management policy used in your agency on use of official time.

The keys to dealing with "reasonable time" provisions are:

☛ Be reasonable but firm in ruling on requests for time;

☛ Be consistent in your decisions.

If there are no past practices and you are interpreting "reasonable" for the first time, remember that your decision will become the starting point for establishing a practice on this subject. So give it some thought rather than making a "spur-of-the-moment" decision.

A Final Note

Our goal in writing this book is not to make you an expert in leave administration. But, once you have read *Managing Leave and Attendance Problems*, you should be more confident in performing this important aspect of your job as a supervisor. And, as we have reminded you throughout the book, don't be afraid to call on your personnel representatives for help. These professionals are employed by your agency to advise you and to make your job easier so you should make use of this valuable resource.

About the Authors

Dennis K. Reischl is Director of FPMI Communications, Inc. Prior to founding FPMI, he advised and represented management at the General Services Administration, Office of Personnel Management, Department of the Navy and the Wisconsin Electric Power Company. He has authored a number of articles and books on the federal personnel system. He is also co-editor of two newsletters: *The Federal Labor & Employee Relations Update* and *The Federal Manager's Edge*.

Robert J. Gilson is Associate Director of the Federal Personnel Management Institute, Inc. He is the author of *The Federal Manager's Guide to EEO* and a co-author of *The Federal Employee's Guide to Drug Testing* and *The Federal Supervisor's Guide to Drug Testing*. Bob has more than twenty years of experience in labor and employee relations. He has advised and represented management at the Department of the Navy, Office of Personnel Management, and Department of the Army. He has spoken at federal conferences and training seminars throughout the United States.

Training Seminars Available from FPMI

The Federal Personnel Management Institute, Inc. specializes in training seminars for Federal managers and supervisors. These seminars can be conducted at your worksite at a per person rate that is substantially less than open enrollment seminars.

The instructors for FPMI seminars have all had practical experience with the Federal Government and know problems Federal supervisors face and how to deal effective with those problems.

Some of the seminar-workshops available include:

• "Managing Unionized Employees Effectively"

• "Developing Effective Performance Standards"

• "Managing Problem Employees"

• "Basic Labor Relations Workshop"

• "Negotiations Workshop"

• "Managing Labor Relations Conflict"

• "Preventing Sexual Harassment"

• "Managing Cultural Diversity"

• "Effective EEO Leadership"

• "Legal Writing for Non-Lawyers

• "Handling ULP Disputes"

• "Conducting Fact-Finding and Administrative Investigations"

• "Petitions, Elections and Bargaining Unit Exclusions"

For more training information, call (205) 539-1850 or fax (205) 539-0911

Publications from
FPMI Communications, Inc.

Publications :

The Federal Manager's Survival Guide ($8.95)

• *Writing Effectively for Feds ($8.95)*

• *The Federal Manager's Guide To Liability ($8.95)*

• *Managing the Civilian Work Force* ($8.95)

• *Practical Ethics for the Federal Employee (2nd Ed.)* ($8.95)

• *The Federal Manager's Guide to TQM* ($8.95)

• *The Federal Manager's Guide to EEO (2nd Ed.)* ($8.95)

• *Managing Leave and Attendance Problems:*

A Guide for the Federal Supervisor ($8.95)

The Federal Manager's Guide to

Preventing Sexual Harassment (2nd Ed.) ($8.95)

• *Sexual Harassment and the Federal Employee (2nd Ed.) ($4.95)*

• *The Federal Supervisor's Guide to Drug Testing (2nd Ed.)* ($8.95)

• *The Supervisor's Guide to Federal Labor Relations (2nd Ed.)* ($8.95)

• *The Federal Manager's Guide to Discipline (2nd ed.)* ($8.95)

• *Performance Standards Made Simple!: A Practical Guide for Federal*
   Managers and Supervisors (3rd Ed.) ($8.95)

Publications for Practitioners
• *Federal Employment Law Practitioner's Handbook (1992-93)* ($59.95)

• *The Desktop Guide to Handling ULP's* ($35.00)

• *The Practitioner's Guide to Federal Sector Negotiability* ($35.00)

• *The Union Representative's Guide to Federal Labor Relations* ($8.95)

Shipping
1-10 Books: $3.50, 11-50 Books: $10.00, 51+: Actual UPS Shipping
Quantity discounts available. For more information or to place an order
(205) 539-1850 or fax (205) 539-0911
Prices effective through December 31, 1993

Videotapes and Newsletters
from FPMI Communications, Inc.

Videotapes:

• *Dealing With Misconduct*
>   Package includes video program, 25 guidebooks and 25 copies of
>   *Federal Manager's Guide to Discipline* for $695.00

• *Writing Effective Performance Standards*
>   Package includes video program, 25 guidebooks and 25 copies of
>   *Performance Standards Made Simple!* for $695.00

• *Managing Under a Labor Agreement*
• *Managing Under The Labor Relations Law*
>   Special package includes both video programs with 25 workbooks for each
>   course and 25 copies of *The Supervisors Guide to Federal Labor
>   Relations* for $895.00. Additional workbooks $5.00 each.

• *Sexual Harassment: Not Government Approved*
• *Preventing Sexual Harassment: Some Practical Answers*
>   Order separate courses for $495.00 each. Or purchase our special
>   package of both video programs with 25 workbooks and a Leader's
>   Guide, 25 copies of *The Federal Supervisors Guide to
>   Preventing Sexual Harassment* and *Sexual Harassment and The
>   Federal Employee* for $895.00.

Monthly Newsletters:

• *The Federal Labor & Employee Relations Update*

>   12 month subscription $195

• *The MSPB Alert*
>   12 months $125.00
>   (Subscribe to both the *The Federal Labor & Employee Relations
>   Update* **and** *The MSPB Alert* at the same time and receive *The
>   Alert* for only$95.00 per year)

The Federal EEO Update
>   12 month subscription $145

• *The Federal Manager's Edge*
>   12 month subscription $65.00

To order or for information on quantity discounts, call FPMI
Communications on (205) 539-1850 or fax (205) 539-0911

Prices effective through December 31, 1993

The Federal Manager's Edge

The monthly newsletter from FPMI Communications that keeps Federal managers and supervisors up-to-date on case decisions that affect the Federal workforce and the role of the Federal manager.

Each issue contains new case decisions, personnel tips and management guidance on a variety of topics from labor relations and ethics to recent holdings of the comptroller general, the Merit Systems Protection Board and the Equal Employment Opportunity Commission that affect you and your agency.

Edge subscriptions are only $65.00 per year (12 issues) and quantity discounts are available to enable your agency to provide copies for all managers and supervisors.

To start your subscription or to receive a complimentary review copy of the *Edge*, just fax the enclosed form to FPMI Communications on (205) 539-0911 or send it to:

FPMI Communications, Inc.
707 Fiber Street
Huntsville, Alabama 35801